D1341912

A Book of Childhood Prayers and Verses

Also compiled by Carolyn Martin:

A Book of Graces

A BOOK OF CHILDHOOD PRAYERS AND VERSES

Compiled by
Carolyn Martin

Illustrations by
Andy Martin

Hodder & Stoughton

LONDON SYDNEY AUCKLAND

The quotation on page 5 is taken from 'God to be first serv'd' by Robert Herrick (1591–1674).

A cataloguing in publication record is available from the British Library

ISBN 0-340-56763-5

Published by Hodder and Stoughton, a division of Hodder and Stoughton Ltd, Mill Road, Dunton Green, Sevenoaks, Kent TN13 2YA. Editorial Office: 47 Bedford Square, London WC1B 3DP.

Designed by Dixon & Jodel
Photoset by Rowland Phototypesetting Ltd, Bury St Edmunds, Suffolk
Printed in Great Britain by Butler and Tanner Ltd, Frome, Somerset

Honour thy Parents;
*   but good manners call*
Thee to adore thy God,
*   the first of all.*

CONTENTS

ACKNOWLEDGMENTS

The compiler and publishers are grateful to the following for permission to include prayers and verses in this anthology:

Associated Book Publishers Ltd, for a prayer by Wilhelmina Stitch.
Associated Book Publishers Ltd, McClelland & Stewart Ltd, Toronto, and E. P. Dutton Inc. (copyright 1924 by E. P. Dutton & Co., Inc., renewal 1952, for a poem from *When We Were Very Young* by A. A. Milne. Reprinted by permission of the publisher, E. P. Dutton, Inc.).
Estate of the late G. K. Chesterton and A. P. Watt Ltd as its representative, for two poems by G. K. Chesterton.
The Collect for the Twenty-fifth Sunday after Trinity, from the Book of Common Prayer of 1662, which is Crown Copyright, is reproduced by permission.
The Guildford Museum, for verses from the following samplers:
  'Teach me to feel another's woe . . .'
  'Humility I'd recommend . . .'
Oxford University Press, for an extract from *Lark Rise to Candleford* by Flora Thompson, 1945.
Prayer for Peace, The Caravan, 197 Piccadilly, London W1, for 'An International Prayer for Peace' by Jain, adapted from the Upanishads.
United Nations Women's Guild, for 'The Children's Charter' by Dorothy Roigt from *Ride with the Sun*, 1955.

I am also indebted to Mrs E. Edmunds for the Welsh translation.

Every effort has been made to trace and contact the owners of copyright material. If there are any inadvertent omissions in the acknowledgments, the compiler apologises to those concerned.

PREFACE

Nostalgia has become one of the characteristics of our times. Victorian and Edwardian journals attract worldwide attention and the wartime reminiscences of 'ordinary' families are read with enthusiasm. Faced with an uncertain future, we cling to our certain and familiar past.

One custom that has declined over the years is the practice of saying family prayers. Many old people look back with affection on their childhood prayers, said 'at mother's knee'. Older people usually remember their childhood verses far more accurately than prayers learnt in later life. Often, from habit, the verses have been repeated nightly since childhood or they have been recalled to mind by specific events.

In this abridged and revised anthology, originally published in 1983, I have tried to collect verses that are alive in so many memories and may eventually be lost to us all.

How many people remember a favourite framed picture from childhood? If this happens to contain a prayer, the memory is even more poignant. The words may not be understood at the time but the image survives. Similarly, embroidered samplers, with appropriately edifying verses or prayers, were studied and worked on for years by young children before being proudly displayed on the wall. We have a rich heritage of samplers in our museums and in private homes and the verses are a valuable, if occasionally morbid, source of prayer.

The emphasis of this book is on prayers from the past but, as an added interest, some more modern prayers, formal school prayers and poetry have been included. As a book for adults and children, I hope that reading it will stimulate interest in childhood prayers and that in time some of the old traditions will be revived. Prayers, like fashions, come and go, but their intrinsic value remains.

Thanks

I must thank the many correspondents who have written to me. Their letters, containing well-loved childhood prayers, have been a real inspiration and a delight to read. The following letter is typical of many.

> Your request opened up a floodgate of memories for me. I found myself singing this little prayer last night over and over again. Even if you do not have use for it in your collection, I wish to thank you for giving me the opportunity of recalling my very early childhood.

All such letters have helped to make this book a collection of living prayers and, generally, the name of the contributor has been placed after the prayer.

In addition, I am grateful for help from the staff at the Victoria and Albert Museum, the Guildford Museum and the Welsh Folk Museum, to Miss Alix Joseph for the loan of many early books of children's prayers, and to my husband who is always my best critic.

Carolyn Martin
Carlidnack, 1992

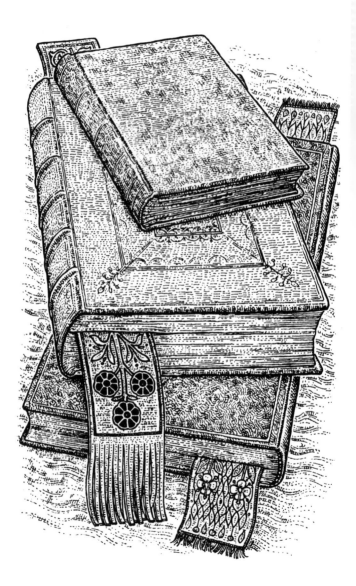

OLDER PRAYERS

A Child's Prayer
Dr Isaac Watts (1674–1748) wrote primarily for
children and Song XX from *Divine and Moral Songs for
Children*, first published in 1715, has become part of
our folklore.

Song XX

Against Idleness and Mischief

How doth the little busy bee
Improve each shining hour,
And gather honey all the day
From every opening flower!

How skilfully she builds her cell!
How neat she spreads the wax!
And labours hard to store it well
With the sweet food she makes.

In works of labour or of skill,
I would be busy too;
For Satan finds some mischief still
For idle hands to do.

In books, or works, or healthful play,
Let my first years be past,
That I may give for every day
Some good account at last.

A Prayer taught by a Notre Dame Nun, eighty
years ago

> Dear little Jesus, come to me.
> Dear little Jesus, stay with me.
> My heart is so small,
> Thou fillest it all.
> There is room for no one,
> But only thee.
> Dear little Jesus, come to me.

(Mrs Winifred Luceman)

A Verse from *Universal Prayer*
By Alexander Pope (1688–1744).

> Teach me to feel another's woe,
>   To hide the fault I see;
> That mercy I to others show,
>   That mercy show to me.

(Sarah Oates, 1788, Low Hall)

A Prayer from *Lark Rise to Candleford*
Flora Thompson (1876–1947), recording her life in rural
Oxfordshire, remembers some children still saying the
following prayer before going to bed.

> Matthew, Mark, Luke and John,
> Bless the bed where I lie on.
> Four corners have I to my bed;
> At them four angels nightly spread.
> One to watch and one to pray
> And one to take my soul away.
> (*or* And two to bear my soul away.)

A Poem for Bedtime

Original Poems for Infant Minds published in 1804 by Ann (1782–1866) and Jane Taylor (1783–1824), who both composed many rhymes for children including 'Twinkle, twinkle, little star'.

Going to Bed at Night

Receive my body, pretty bed;
Soft pillow, Oh receive my head;
And thanks, my parents kind,
For comforts you for me provide;
Your precepts still shall be my guide,
Your love I'll keep in mind.

My hours misspent this day I rue;
My good things done, how very few!
Forgive my faults, O Lord;
This night, if in thy grace I rest,
Tomorrow may I rise refreshed,
To keep thy holy word.

(Ms Betty Harris)

Words of Advice by Florence Nightingale (1820–1910)

Live your life while you have it. Life is a splendid gift. There is nothing small in it. For the greatest things grow by God's law out of the smallest.

A Prayer from a Sampler

Samplers are pieces of embroidery worked by young girls as specimens of proficiency. They are often displayed on the wall and were at their most popular during the seventeenth century. Here is the most frequently used sampler verse. It has been attributed to both the Rev. John Newton (1725–1807) and to Dr Isaac Watts (1674–1748), but as the verse does not appear before the 1790s it is more likely to be from the writings of the Rev. John Newton. 1794 is usually given as the earliest date for the verse, but the following has the date 1791–2.

> Jesu permit thy gracious name to stand
> As the first efforts of an infant hand
> And whilst her fingers on the canvas move
> Engage her tender heart to seek thy love
> With thy dear children let her have a part
> And write thy Name thyself upon her heart.

(Mary Schofield of Sheffield, 1791–2)

A Verse from a Sampler in Guildford Museum

> Humility I'd recommend
> Good nature too with ease
> Be generous good and kind to all
> You'll never fail to please
> Be ever thankful to that God
> Whose blessings you receive
> Adore no other God but he
> In him alone believe.

(Mary Stephens, 1818)

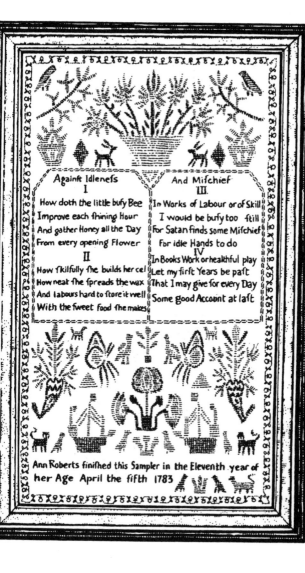

A Prayer by Wilhelmina Stitch

My Prayer is such a little thing, it might get
    lost and go astray.
Are you, dear God, now listening to what I
    say?
I wish to thank You for the sun that kissed, this
    morn, my sleeping eyes;
for all the happy things I've done since I did
    rise.

For gift of sound and gift of sight; for feet that
    skip so merrily;
for food and warmth, and each delight You gave
    to me.
I thank You for my mother dear; I thank You
    for my father kind;
and for the star that watches near – behind the
    blind.

So many Grown-ups show me love, though I'm
    a child and still quite small.
Look down upon them from above – and please
    God, bless them all.
And now, dear God, I'll say, 'Goodnight', and
    may Your angels guard my bed
until You send Your morning light to wake this
    Sleepy Head

*(Miss Marjorie Joseph, who heard Wilhelmina Stitch, a writer of
popular religious verse, at a prayer meeting in Chester, March 1930.)*

A Prayer of Thankfulness

> Next unto God, dear Parents, I address
> Myself to you, in humble thankfulness.
> For all your care and charge on me bestow'd,
> And means of learning unto me allow'd.
> Go on, dear Parents, let me still pursue
> Those golden Arts the vulgar never knew.

Performed by Ann Mann in 1765, aged ten.

(The great-great-grandmother of the contributor, who now lives in Kent.)

Church Prayers and Hymns

From a Hymn by Charles Wesley

'Gentle Jesus' was the first hymn composed by Charles Wesley (1707–88) and it was published in *Hymns and Sacred Poems* in 1742. Usually just the first two verses are remembered.

> Gentle Jesus, meek and mild,
> Look upon a little child;
> Pity my simplicity,
> Suffer me to come to thee.
>
> Fain I would to thee be brought:
> Gracious Lord, forbid it not;
> In the kingdom of thy grace
> Find a little child a place.

A Welsh version of 'Gentle Jesus', translated by Parch W. O. Evans, is still said or sung in schools and homes today.

> Iesu tirion, gwêl yn awr
> Blentyn bach yn plygu i lawr;
> Wrth fy ngwendid trugarha,
> Paid am gwrthod Iesu da.

A Prayer for Children

A prayer by the Rev. C. M. O. Parkinson, Curate at the Church of St Mary the Virgin, Baldock, Hertfordshire, 1882, and found in a child's exercise book under the floorboards of an old house.

> O God, guard, we pray thee, the little children in this place. Preserve their innocency, keep them under the shadow of thy wings, that they may continue thine for ever, and daily grow in grace and holiness, even unto their lives' end.

A Prayer for a Child's Christening

By the Rev. W. T. Wingfield, former Vicar of Rillington, E. Yorks.

> We pray thee to bless this child that as he is
>   thine by creation,
> he also may become thine by adoption and
>   grace.
> To be inside thy loving protection in this world
>   and number him
> with thy faithful servants in the world to come.

(Mr N. A. Hudleston)

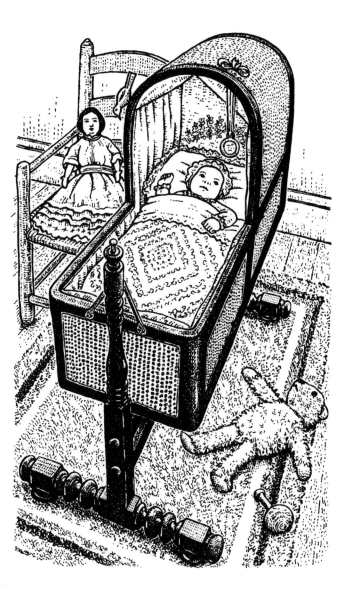

A Prayer for the Holy Spirit

This well-known hymn is based on the words of Bianco da Siena, 1434, and translated by R. F. Littledale.

> Come down, O Love divine,
> Seek thou this soul of mine,
> And visit it with thine own ardour glowing;
> O Comforter, draw near,
> Within my heart appear,
> And kindle it, thy holy flame bestowing.

A Prayer for Evening

This was written in 1839 by Mary L. Duncan (1814–40), three years after her marriage and three months before her untimely death.

> Jesus, tender Shepherd, hear me,
> Bless thy little lamb tonight;
> Through the darkness be thou near me,
> Watch my sleep till morning light.
>
> All this day thy hand has led me,
> And I thank thee for thy care;
> Thou hast clothed me, warmed and fed me,
> Listen to my evening prayer.
>
> Let my sins be all forgiven,
> Bless the friends I love so well;
> Take me, when I die, to heaven,
> Happy there with thee to dwell.

(Mr Harold Binks and Miss Mary Corbett Harris)

A Prayer for 'Stir Up Sunday'

The Collect for the Twenty-fifth Sunday after Trinity, 'Stir Up Sunday', is remembered as the time when, traditionally, many people made a start on their Christmas puddings.

> Stir up, we beseech thee, O Lord, the wills of thy faithful people; that they, plenteously bringing forth the fruit of good works, may of thee be plenteously rewarded; through Jesus Christ our Lord. Amen.

A Prayer by Susan Warner (1819–85)

> Jesus bids us shine
> With a pure clear light,
> Like a little candle
> Burning in the night.
> In this world of darkness;
> So let us shine,
> You in your small corner,
> And I in mine.

Morning and Evening

A Morning Prayer
From Burnt Oak Council School, Edgware.

> Praise God, Oh my soul, for He hath brought
> me to see another day – Heavenly Father, help
> me to live as thy child and to walk in thy ways.
> Teach me to speak the truth, to shun what is
> evil and to do what is good. In all my thoughts,
> words and deeds, may I bear in mind that thou
> God, seest me.
>
> Bless my dear parents and all people, pardon
> my sins and hear my prayer, for Jesus Christ's
> sake. Amen.

*(Mrs N. K. Blay left school in 1909 and estimates that she said this
prayer about 1,600 times!)*

An Ancient Collect, 590 A.D.

> O God, who hast folded back the mantle of the
> night to clothe us in the golden glory of the
> day, chase from our hearts all gloomy
> thoughts, and make us glad with the brightness
> of hope, that we may effectively aspire to
> unwon virtues, through Jesus Christ our Lord.
> Amen.

A Prayer for the End of the Day
This popular prayer was often said at the end of the
school day before leaving for home.

> Lord keep us safe this night,
> Secure from all our fears.
> May Angels guard us while we sleep,
> Till morning light appears. Amen.

*(Mrs L. Barnett was taught the verse seventy-five years ago, at Waterloo
Road School, Manchester.)*

A Prayer Before Sleep
In this prayer the line 'If I should die before I wake' may
seem strange today, but when the prayer first appeared
in a New England Primer in 1781, the fear of early
death, disease and darkness was much more real.

> Now I lay me down to sleep,
> I pray the Lord my soul to keep.
> If I should die before I wake
> I pray the Lord my soul to take.

From 'Vespers'
Taken from *When We Were Very Young* by A. A. Milne
(1882–1956)

> Little Boy kneels at the foot of the bed,
> Droops on the little hands little gold head.
> Hush! Hush! Whisper who dares!
> Christopher Robin is saying his prayers.

A Prayer by Gabriel Setoun (1861–1930)
From *Prayers and Graces* by Dorothy Sheldon.

> God watches o'er us all the day,
> At home, at school and at our play;
> And when the sun has left the skies
> He watches with a million eyes.

(Mrs Rita Roberts)

A Prayer by Bishop Lancelot Andrewes (1555–1626)
The Bishop of Chichester, Ely and Winchester, who was noted for his fine preaching and saintly life.

> Take us, we pray thee, O Lord of our life, into
> thy keeping this night and for ever. O thou
> Light of lights, keep us from inward darkness;
> grant us to sleep in peace, that we may arise to
> work according to thy will: through Jesus
> Christ our Lord. Amen.

'Evening' by G. K. Chesterton (1874–1936)

> Here dies another day
> During which I have had eyes, ears, hands
> And the great world around me.
> And with tomorrow begins another.
> Why am I allowed two?

(From the Most Rev. J. S. Habgood, Archbishop of York, for whom the words breathe an atmosphere of childlike wonder.)

TWO FAMILIAR EVENING PRAYERS

In this little bed I lie,
Heavenly Father, hear my cry,
Lord protect me through the night,
Keep me safe 'till morning light. Amen.

*(Ms Margaret J. Schofield, a prayer taught by her mother and
grandmother)*

Dear Jesus, from thy throne above,
Look down upon thy child with love.
Watch o'er me nightly, hear my prayer,
And keep thy little one with care. Amen.

(Mrs Matilda James, from her childhood, ninety-five years ago)

SCHOOL

THANKS FOR THE GOOD THINGS IN LIFE
Westminster School was founded in 1560. The 'Order of
Prayer for Westminster School' was written by Bishop
Thomas Ken (1637–1711) and sounds distinctly
modern, brimming over with thanks for the good things
in life.

> Giver of all good things, we thank thee: for
> health and vigour; for the air that gives the
> breath of life, the sun that warms us, and the
> good food that makes us strong; for happy
> homes and for the friends we love; for all that
> makes it good to live. Make us thankful and
> eager to repay, by cheerfulness and kindliness,
> and by a readiness to help others. Freely we
> have received; let us freely give, in the name
> of him who gave his life for us, Jesus Christ our
> Lord.
>
> *(Dr John Rae, former Headmaster, Westminster School)*

A Prayer for Protection

Bedales School, Petersfield, Hampshire, was founded in 1893. This prayer was adapted by the Founder, Mr J. G. Baddley, for the Sunday evening service.

> Father of all men, we pray you to watch over those who are about to go forth from our midst to face the unknown battle of life. May they feel that thy loving care is ever with them in all their troubles and perplexities, so that they may come safe through every danger, and grow strong to serve thee all the days of their life.

(Mr C. P. Nobes, former Headmaster of Bedales)

A Prayer for Good Conduct

Monkton Combe Junior School, Bath, was founded in 1888. The School Prayer was written by Canon D. F. Horsefield, who was a member of the teaching staff at the school from 1913–16.

> O God and Father of us all from Whom alone we have the desire and the power to live aright: Grant that the clean page of this new day may remain unspotted to its end; and that whatsoever is recorded upon it by our lives may prove worthy to be treasured in our memories: so that at the day's closing we may present it unashamed to thee: through Jesus Christ our Lord.

(Mr Michael Coates, former Headmaster, Monkton Combe Junior School)

A Prayer before Lessons

Lord God my Heavenly Father, thou art very good to me.

I thank thee for taking care of me through the night and that I am alive and well this morning. Help me today to be a good child and to do what is right. Keep me from wicked thoughts, evil tempers and bad words.

Make me kind and gentle to my companions, honest and true in all I do and say, and attentive to my work in school. Help me to grow better every day and to follow the example of the Holy Jesus, for Jesus Christ's sake. Amen.

(Mrs Rhoda Butler, who left school in 1918, three days before her fourteenth birthday.)

A Prayer from Scotland

Teach me to pray, dear Lord, teach me to pray,
Not only to say my prayers but really to pray.
Others, dear Lord, can tell me what to say,
But only You can lead me on to pray.

(Miss Sarah McQuade was told in school that she would not appreciate this prayer until she was older.)

A Prayer for Grace

I am the child of God
I ought to do His will
I can do what he tells me to
And by His grace I will.

(Mrs Sybil Harton)

A Prayer from Wales
A prayer from Aberdyberthi Sunday School, Swansea,
spoken as the children left for home.

Now before we homeward go,
Father listen to our prayer.
We thy children here below,
Come to ask thy tender care.

Soon this happy day will end,
Night clouds cover all the sky;
Jesus, little children's friend,
Guard us while asleep we lie.

Then through all the hours of night,
Safe and happy we shall be.
For we know that dark and light,
Both are just alike to thee. Amen.

(Mr George Morris)

HOME AND FAMILY

A MOTHERING SUNDAY PRAYER FROM A CHILD OF SIX

Thank you God for our Grannies,
for without them,
we would not have had our Mummies.

(Rev. Canon James S. Robertson)

'TELL ME, TELL ME' BY EMILY JANE BRONTË
(1818–48)
Although best known as the author of *Wuthering
Heights*, this illustrates her gift for poetry.

Tell me, tell me, smiling child,
What the past is like to thee?
'An autumn evening, soft and mild,
With a wind that sighs mournfully.'

Tell me, what is the present hour?
'A green and flowery spray,
Where a young bird sits gathering its power
To mount and fly away.'

And what is the future, happy one?
'A sea beneath a cloudless sun –
A mighty, glorious, dazzling sea,
Stretching into infinity.'

A Child's Poem
As recorded by a seven-year-old schoolgirl, thirty years ago.

Lines of Comfort

God made a little garden
For every little child,
In it he planted laughter
And fun to grow there wild,
And then he sowed some kindness
Near little sprigs of hope,
And scattered seeds of friendship
To bloom on love's warm slope.

And then God left one corner
In every child's own care
To plant His loveliest flower,
Its name is little prayer.
It takes root in a whisper,
It blossoms night and day,
Its scent goes up to heaven
And it never fades away.

*(Miss Enid Beaumont, Headmistress of Little Reddings Infants School,
Bushey, Hertfordshire)*

'TIME'S PACES' BY REV. HENRY TWELLS
(1823–1900)
The Rev. Henry Twells was Rector of Baldock,
Hertfordshire, and Waltham-on-the-Wolds,
Leicestershire. This poem can be found printed on the
front of a clock-case in the North Transept of Chester
Cathedral.

> When as a child I laughed and wept,
>   Time crept.
> When as a youth I waxed more bold,
>   Time strolled.
> When I became a full-grown man,
>   Time RAN.
> When older still I daily grew,
>   Time FLEW.
> Soon I shall find, in passing on,
>   Time gone.
> O Christ! wilt thou have saved me then?
>   Amen.

A PRAYER FOR FATHERS
Written by children aged from four to thirteen in Leeds.

> Dear Lord,
> Please look after all fathers when they have to
>   go away on meetings.
> Help fathers not to work too hard, otherwise
>   they suffer from exhaustion.
> Let fathers know how much we love them.

(Mrs Margaret Wrench)

A Prayer for a Grandmother

An amused grandmother contributed the following from her six-year-old grand-daughter:

> Please God take great care of Granny,
> and let her go on living till she is very old,
> and when she can't cook any more –
> then you can have her!

(Lady Anderson)

A Prayer for Children

By Gerald Priestland, formerly the BBC's Religious Affairs Correspondent.

> God my father, God my mother,
> God my sister, God my brother,
> God my enemy and friend.
> My beginning and my end:
> God in every beast and tree,
> Thank you for the best in me.

A BOY'S PRAYER
By Henry Charles Beeching, from a parish magazine in
Derbyshire, dated 1901.

> God who created me
> Nimble and light of limb,
> In three elements free,
> To run, to ride, to swim:
> Not when the sense is dim,
> But now from the heart of joy,
> Take the thanks of a boy.

(Rev. A. C. F. Nicoll)

MODERN PRAYERS

A PRAYER OF STRUGGLE
By a ten-year-old girl from St Anne's School,
Windermere.

Please God help me today. I have so many
worries. I worry about my home and family
with its problems, my school and work,
whether I am doing the right thing. The exams
are coming soon, will I do well? Am I nice to
everyone I meet? Why was I so mean and
nasty in things I did today?

I know I've experienced that you can help
solve problems. I have hope and faith in you.
You can put things right when they go wrong.

Please Lord make me try hard and do
everything thoroughly and do the best I can.
Today I felt hatred against people. I want to
rebel. I know I should be kinder, but it's
difficult Lord. Help me please.

A PRAYER FOR PROTECTION

From ghouls and ghosties and long-leggety
beasties
And things that go bump in the night;
Good Lord deliver us.

*(The Rt Rev. John Yates, Bishop of Gloucester, vividly remembers
repeating this litany to himself to combat his childhood fears at night.)*

A SIMPLE PRAYER
By an eleven-year-old pupil from Walthamstow Hall,
Sevenoaks, Kent.

> God bless Mummy,
> God bless Daddy,
> God bless Bruce,
> God bless Loki (Cat),
> God bless Tiggy (Dead Cat),
> God bless George and Pepper (Dead Guinea
>   Pigs),
> God bless everyone and
> God bless me. Amen.

TROUBLE AT SCHOOL
A prayer by an eleven-year-old girl from Clocaenog
County Primary School, Ruthin, Clwyd.

> Dear Jesus when I feel bad about things in
> school and go quiet, I try and tell you things,
> but it is difficult because children call me,
> teachers call me and I cannot concentrate and
> so these things hover round until I go to bed.
> Then when I tell you these things I feel much
> better. Jesus thank you for making me feel
> better. Amen.

THE TEENAGER'S PRAYER

> O God, give me patience.
> And I want it right now.

(Rt Rev. Michael Mann, former Dean of Windsor)

A Prayer by Cardinal Cushing (1895–1970)
Former Archbishop of Boston, Massachusetts.

> If all the sleeping will wake up,
> all the lukewarm folk will fire up,
> all the crooked will straighten up,
> all the depressed folk will cheer up,
> all the estranged folk will make up,
> all the gossip folk will shut up,
> all the dry bones will shake up,
> and the true believers stand up,
> all the church members show up
> To honour Him who was lifted up,
> ·Then we can have the world's greatest
> Renewal.

A Prayer for Help
Written by an eleven-year-old boy from St Aubyns,
Brighton.

The Flight Prayer

> Dear Lord, give us clearance on the runway to
> thy world. Steer us free from the low cloud of
> temptation. Keep us on thy course and help us
> to stay at a humble height, not to fly too low
> and not to fly too high and, if our engines fail,
> give us fuel to revive them and, at the end,
> guide us to our destination with thee. Through
> Jesus Christ our Lord. Amen.

Words by G. K. Chesterton (1874–1936)

> The Snail does the Holy
> Will of God slowly.

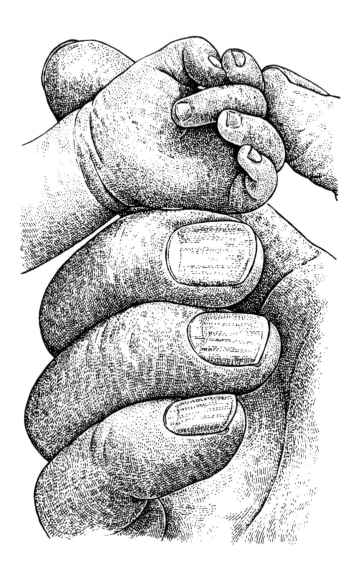

PRAYERS FOR OTHERS

THE PRAYER OF THE SIOUX INDIANS

> O Great Spirit, help me never to judge another
> until I have walked two weeks in his
> moccasins.

A GYPSY PROVERB

> If people do not know much, do not laugh at
>   them,
> for every one of them knows something that
>   you do not know.

FROM *MORTE D'ARTHUR*
By Alfred Lord Tennyson (1809–92)

> More things are wrought by prayer
> Than this world dreams of.

FOR BROWNIES

> O God our Father, help us to love others
> before ourselves and to love thee most of all.
> Keep us from love of our own way. Give us
> busy hands, loving hearts, and minds eager to
> learn. Make us always happy in making others
> happy, especially in our homes and in the Pack;
> through Jesus Christ our Lord.

A Prayer for Compassion

The physically handicapped children of the Victoria
School, Poole, Dorset, have their own booklet of
prayers written by the children.

> Heavenly Father, we pray today that you will
> help us to help old people, also people who are
> lonely. Please help us to feel like being helpful
> all the time. Even if we are doing something
> and we don't want to be bothered by anybody.
> Dear God hear this prayer for Jesus' sake.
> Amen.

A 'Thinking Day' Prayer

By Julie Pye, a fourteen-year-old Queen's Guide. The
prayer was written for a Girl Guide Thinking Day
Service in Staffordshire.

> Dear Lord,
>
> In the garden, cool and green,
> The strong supporting cane is seen.
> This garden cane, so tall and straight,
> Supports the frailer flowers' weight.
> There it stands, tall and strong,
> Supporting beauty all day long.
> Lord, make us like the garden cane,
> Supporting people just the same,
> Supporting those who may be frail
> Or maybe weak, and so may fail.
> Then, like the delicate carnation,
> Which is weaker than the rest,
> But, given tender love and care,
> It often blooms the best.

(Mr John M. Day, General Secretary, Independent Methodist Churches)

AN INTERNATIONAL PRAYER FOR PEACE

A non-denominational prayer which people around the world were asked to voice or meditate on at mid-day, local time. The prayer was offered until the second special session on Disarmament at the United Nations in June 1982.

> Lead me from death
> To life, from falsehood to truth.
>
> Lead me from despair
> To hope, from fear to trust.
>
> Lead me from hate
> To love, from war to peace.
>
> Let peace fill our heart,
> Our world, our universe.

(Rev. David M. Lindsay)

THE CHILDREN'S CHARTER

By Dorothy Roigt, founder of the United Nations Women's Guild in 1948.

> There shall be peace on earth, but not until
> All children daily eat their fill,
> Go warmly clad against the winter wind
> And learn their lessons with a tranquil mind.
>
> And thus released from hunger, fear and need,
> Regardless of their colour, race or creed,
> Look upward smiling to the skies,
> Their faith in life reflected in their eyes.

Classic Prayers

A Prayer by St Clement (a.d. 96)
The third Bishop of Rome after St Peter; his feast day
is celebrated on 23rd November.

> O God, make us children of quietness, and
> heirs of peace.

A Prayer by St Augustine of Hippo (345–430)
From *The Junior House Prayer Book* of Ampleforth
College, York (founded 1802). St Augustine was
appointed Bishop of Hippo (North Africa) in 396.

> O God, from whom to be turned is to fall,
> to whom to be turned is to rise,
> and in whom to stand is to abide for ever:
> Grant us in all our duties your help,
> in all our perplexities your guidance,
> in all our dangers your protection,
> and in all our sorrows your peace,
> through Jesus Christ our Lord.

(Rev. D. L. Milroy, O.S.B., Headmaster, Ampleforth College)

A Prayer by St Ignatius Loyola (1491–1556)

Teach us, good Lord,
To serve thee as thou deservest;
To give and not to count the cost;
To fight and not to heed the wounds;
To toil and not to seek for rest;
To labour and not to ask for any reward
Save that of knowing that we do thy will.

(Miss G. W. Combes)

In Praise of God
By Gerard Manley Hopkins (1844–89). Much of his
poetry was only published after his death, when
collected together by Robert Bridges.

Pied Beauty

Glory be to God for dappled things –
For skies of couple-colour as a brinded cow;
For rose-moles all in stipple upon trout that
    swim;
Fresh-firecoal chestnut-falls; finches' wings;
Landscape plotted and pieced – fold, fallow,
    and plough;
All all trades, their gear and tackle and trim.

All things counter, original, spare, strange;
Whatever is fickle, freckled (who knows how?)
With swift, slow; sweet, sour; adazzle, dim;
He fathers-forth whose beauty is past change:
Praise him.

TIME PASSING
By Edgar Allan Poe (1809–49) who was born in Boston, Massachusetts, but attended school in England.

A Dream Within A Dream

I stand amid the roar
Of a surf-tormented shore,
And I hold within my hand
Grains of the golden sand –
How few! yet how they creep
Through my fingers to the deep,
While I weep – while I weep!
O God! can I not grasp
Them with a tighter clasp?
O God! can I not save
One from the pitiless wave?
Is *all* that we see or seem
But a dream within a dream?

A MOTHER'S ADVICE
A prayer adapted from the familiar lines in Shakespeare's *Hamlet*, Act I, Scene III.

Remember, to your own self be true,
Treat all mankind with kindness and dignity.
They are formed in God's image,
And God will require an answer.
Be faithful to your prayers and
If I don't meet you all here on earth,
We'll surely meet in Heaven.

(Mrs Mary Brigid Mullen)

LAST LINES
A verse from 'Pippa Passes' by Robert Browning
(1812–89)

> The year's at the spring,
> And day's at the morn;
> Morning's at seven;
> The hill-side's dew-pearled;
> The lark's on the wing;
> The snail's on the thorn;
> God's in His heaven –
> All's right with the world.

Index of FIRST PHRASES